because God loves the wasp

Elisabeth Blair

Attention schools and businesses: for discounted copies on large orders, please contact the publisher directly.

For information contact:
Unsolicited Press
Portland, Oregon
www.unsolicitedpress.com
orders@unsolicitedpress.com
619-354-8005

Cover Design: Kathryn Gerhardt
Cover photo provided by Elisabeth Blair
Editor: Jay Kristensen Jr. and S.R. Stewart

ISBN: 978-1-956692-28-0

This book documents the author's experience of living for two and a half years in two abusive facilities for so-called troubled teens: Ascent and Rocky Mountain Academy. Both were part of the CEDU Family of Services, which operated from 1967 to 2005. CEDU's programs were based on the harmful teachings and tenets of the mid-century cult Synanon. As this book goes to press, offshoots of CEDU as well as many similar programs continue to operate in the US and abroad, largely unregulated.

I.

SIX WEEKS

Your blanket is the shell of an egg:
You—
young, raw.

You're standing on it.

The man with the handcuffs is generous.
He gives you time.

He helps.

Gets oxygen to your brain,
makes your breast heave—

                                               a bird
                                               on a stoop
                                               on its back
                                               in shock—

Get in the man's truck.

A bone tucked in weeds,
you breathe through hair.

A bean, you're obedient,
plucked from the pod,
shapely on the plate.

Soon you'll deliver your babies
—your voice and testimony—
into their fields, then watch them
be plowed under
from the shelter of a ditch.

They'll pay you in nightmares
for as long as you live.
It's helpful.
It's love.
You'll see, when you're older,
if you make it.

For now, darkness.
Child locks.

Wheeled up switchbacks,
you're fixed, an insect in sap.

Now you're pulled out
into a plywood room.
A woman confiscates your clothes.

A little curtain—that's nice—
the men won't see your breasts and ass,
or wouldn't, but the woman stands
where it should be drawn,
an insufficient human curtain.

She asks if you've ever cut yourself,
demands you show her where.

She knows what you are;
she's seen things like you before.

At 2:00 a.m., you're mixed into a
spread of sleeping girls.

Lie down.
Avert your eyes.

You are not to look anywhere
but the furrows where the
fetuses are.

Because God loves the wasp,
He causes the pear to fall
and meet its lover.

God does not mind the suffering of the girl
who, with a bite, interrupts
the lovers' tryst,

because, in the end, He just
loves the wasp
most.

You wake to hear the staff shout *5 MINUTES* and you're meant to
leap up stuff sleeping bag duffel dress yourself *in agreement* the right
order of layers buttons laces zippers up rain gear on tightly drawn
back hair make all *plumb and square* sweep out to make a circle
heel to heel toe to toe be silent eyes down and do all of this in five
minutes

but no one's told you this. You don't even know which state this is.

Your questions are fungus
on a dead thing;
your being good is not
in the plan. You break their
agreements; you can't not.
What's wrong with her,

a girl whispers. Her transgression
(speech) is less; she's safe while
you're the spectacle,
with your snot and gasps.
It doesn't take them long—
one hour and you've been taught:

     Your self

     must be

on the deck, then run to the mess tent and sit in your designated

put down

spot if anyone speaks or makes eye contact staff explodes with

by either

mockery and abuse now run to the potties again to mock brush

their

your teeth then to the wood corral to saw and chop wood

or your

without instruction now pick up a log and carry it and run

hands—

in your snow and rain gear despite the clear sky then do squats

mercy-

in circuits holding bundles of wood until your knees give out

killed,

then back to the mess tent for mock dinner then mock potties

or at least

undress mock bed again then up get dressed and on and on 40 days'

made to play

schedules in one and this is how you learn what's going on

dead.

The girls ask,
Why are you here?

Your hands spread,
sloughing off pseudo-wholesome milk
—platitudes and sentiments in which
they give you cold baths—
already gathered along your lines.

"I don't know," you respond.
The girls watch you drip.
A mess.

You tell them you're a
slice of grass where a shadow falls—
your greens *seem* burnt
but they're not.

They don't believe it.
You're burned, they say, and you did it yourself.
You're narrowed, scraped away to almost nothing,
and it's how you meant to be:
We are each the sum of our own choices only.

[A is here because
she ran away after her
stepfather raped her]

No one ends up here by accident,
they explain, holding your hands up and
out like theirs, helping you plug
into the mainframe,

[B was in the backseat
when boys shot bullets
from the car]

a lapless lake of guilt and shame.
No one here is innocent.

[C had smoked a single cigarette]

They circle, crescendo, climax,
then advise the staff:
At least to begin with,
you're bulimic.

Straightaway, your *potty privileges* are removed:

In daytime,
you cannot use the bathroom
(the hole in the ground)
on your own,

and at night you have to count out loud
1, 2, 3, 4, 5, 6, 7
while a kind woman from town
working night shift for a coalition of
abusive men and women
listens to you piss.

You think, *at least
they haven't shaved
my head.*

[I am not ungrateful
I am not ungrateful]

Two weeks have passed.

You give a speech to
the children and staff
in hopes of getting your
potty privileges back:

>   *I promise I can be trusted*

>   *with the loan of my*

>   *body*

You're in a sleeping bag. It's been a week.
By now, you know what will be asked, but
you can't begin early—they'll hear,
or the girls will rat.

You'll have to wait.
Voices outside laugh.

All the staff are bullies, but one man
and one woman have something missing:
no organ for breath.

Instead of breathing in, they mock.
Instead of breathing out, they laugh.

On a whim, they'll make a girl dig a grave,
move the dirt 50 feet, then move it back,
and they laugh.

In the mornings, it's possible to be calm
as you wait for the now-familiar scream
that pulls you up from doll to marionette,

but if you hear those two,
you graduate differently,

from doll to cartoon:
chattering teeth, shaking limbs

—and yes,
when they see you,
they'll laugh.

You're on your knees in the snow
with what hope you've grown
over 16 years, trying to share it
with another girl's 13 years' worth.

The man with something missing has left
because the girl couldn't carry her half
and collapsed.

You have to make her stand
so she can help you haul it—
food for 40 children in a metal box
slung from a 2x4, one end
on your shoulder, the other on hers—
through a dark half-mile
in snow above the knees.

An hour of falling, cajoling,
pleading, holding, hugging, and
wiping cakes of snow from your eyes
before you arrive to be presented
to a silent mass of hungry kids.

She's so young, her lips tremble
with each name he calls her, as he

displays the two *disgusting things*,
and tries to teach you who you are—

> *useless victims*
> *pathetic brats*
> *fucking babies*

—but you, you're just old enough
to translate:
He's teaching you who he is.

The sounds are dull.

Maybe if the dishes were metal—
but they're not. They're wood,
woven and pressed.

The staff woman is thorough,
picks each off their shelves—
fifty wooden bowls and plastic cups.

They hit the walls, skid on the floor,
stop under the sink. They don't break
or make proper sounds
(just thuds and tinkles),

YOU   DIDN'T

DRY   THEM
         but *she*
         does.
    ENOUGH

YOU'RE   TRYING

TO   MAKE
         You keep
  US   ALL
         your eyes
         down
    SICK

I

WON'T and find BE
what life
TREAT there is ED

LIKE THIS

PICK THEM

OFF in the THE
breaths
FLOOR between YOU
her
CON- screams. NIVING

BITCH

You only speak when spoken to by the staff,
but the English boy speaks at will. He laughs,

pulls his pants down, and shits
in the mess tent. You look at the grain
in the rough wooden bench.

He kicks as they tackle him to the ground,
and all the while—as they swear and shout
and he fights—comes that laughter,
making ripples in your eyes.

They put him in a sleeping bag,
wrap a tarp around it, tie it with rope,
then leave him on the ground for days,
on display, in March, in the mountains,
in many feet of snow.

They call it a *burrito*.

    Let him laugh,

they say,

    let him wiggle and roll.

                    [we were not killed]

                    [I am not ungrateful
                    I am not ungrateful]

[new truth #2]

I was 16, am now 36,
am only ever surprised
by kindness.

The psychiatrist visits
once a week, gives
ten minutes each to a
handful of kids.

When it's your turn, he says,

> *You were unhappy at home,*
> *and now you don't want to be here.*
> *Do you see the pattern?*
> *You are unhappy wherever you are.*

(Before all this, your parents took you to a therapist.
When you refused to speak and cried mutely on
his couch, he gave them his porcelain-pure, Styrofoam
advice—to hire people to come into your bedroom,
fly you to another state, remove your clothes, then
dress you again in a yarn that absolves these sins.)

He hands you a pen.

Make me a drawing of anything you want—
ah, yes, a princess.

No, just a woman wearing interesting clothes.

Based on this, I'll make a recommendation
to your parents about whether or not
you ought to go on from this six-week hell
to its financially affiliated
two-and-a-half-year prison.

Of course he'll recommend you go on;
of course he has your parents' trust.
A doctor always knows what's best.

II.

TWENTY-EIGHT MONTHS

Fear can be simple

("do not kill me, oh man with a gun")

or can have subtleties,

involve hope

and measuring.

Hope:

to avoid, prolong, shorten, change, maintain—

whatever it is you need to do, hope can take you

through the steps more efficiently than despair.

Measuring:

the intricate moods of Authority.

Miscalculation can result in deaths.

Not from guns—

[I am not ungrateful

I am not ungrateful]

—but other ones:

the three-month death your friend lived through

without eye contact or a friendly word exchanged

with a single soul

even while sitting amongst you all.

You were complicit

in this act of erasure;

you too ignored her.

She ceased to be, except

in the corner of the dining room

at dinner, sitting on her own

along the wall, not allowed

to look, speak, laugh, draw, or smile.

Hers a death you couldn't bear,

so you measured and measured.

You measured and measured.

You measured and measured.

You measured and measured.

You measured and measured.

You sit in a circle of girls.

One tugs, then reveals a war
she once began of hand vs. arm.
Capillaries burst over her eyes
as she screams, making new
violence while confessing old.

                                        [newer is better]

It's your first time
in the mouths of their Gods—
Thoreau, Lennon; the mouth above
America's bootstrapping jaw.

as, need everything

Caught in their
confessed   you must
        teeth like this
you must   you must   you must   you must you must
you must you must you must you must you must you must you must

you, too learn to scream

Your body appears, seated on a couch.

On either side of your head:
a conch shell and an empty space,
respectively.

What does the shell say?
Reveal the noise to us.

You make a mouth shape and do the noise as it is—
benign, insignificant.

We don't believe this is all.
Show us more.

You look and find that you can lift the conch's skirt.
You reveal the ankles and legs of the noise.

But we know that's not all.

They're impatient now. You'd best feed their

mustached, forty-something mouths.

The children in the circle

pull at the wires. Maybe they'll

be kind, maybe they'll pull hard.

You can't know.

You break the conch over your knee and

make your body into a shell,

crying from the pain of condensing and

growing hard. You become a vessel, a

mouth that is now an ear.

WE KNOW THERE IS MORE THAN ONE SHELL!

You pause, uncertain now.

You can't immediately come up with what they want.

There is no other shell, you say,

just empty space.

You're defiant now, and safe in logic and facts,

but the scene blurs as the volume

becomes a storm.

You're wormy, crouching, searching

among the rubble on the floor

for another (perhaps a baby) shell.

Here! A piece of fuzz whose shape resembles a snail.

You present it to the storm,

hold it up from where you kneel,

your eyes flush with salt,

the room misty with spittle and rage

from the mustached spine

and the children beside him.

You scream:

Here's the shell you said would be here—

it's in the shape of a vulva, and means:

me being touched by a boy

and my touching him,

and all the   all   the all the   all   the

shame.

The storm stops.

Wings extend, wrap around you.

You cry with relief. You've performed well.

There will be more—three times a week—

but today you've passed. For now at least

you'll be permitted to speak

and be spoken to (permitted

to be).

The storm wants specific things.

You, poet, can be convincing.

Spare no valuable time or energy

for those who cannot proceed

with the academic rigor, dramatic

skill, and creativity necessary.

Tell no one.

Be absolutely alone,

but be.

How it feels is a series of questions:

Are you home now, or in the body of an animal?

Do you drown, or do you sit calm
in the watery air?
And the fire—did you light it yourself, or
did someone you know, or someone
you have yet to meet?

Can you sit quiet by it
or is it bridging the wet and dry with its feet,
consuming your shoes first, then your eyes,
skipping the topography in between
in fickle pecking
like chicken for grain?

Is the shower water or is it fire?

What if you want to feel
something?

Are you tired of time, to be so locked into now
in this way, in the shower, and later
in the circle, where they'll say,

> *We saw your scars, we know you were abused—*
> *it's okay—we were too—*

—? But you had only scratched your back
in the shower (accidentally) that day.

What is the fire that is the fire of drowning
and what is the urgency that is the command of fog,
saying you'd better sit down?
You'd better stand up.

Wood. Upholstery. Snow. Mud.
These are real, while you are sinister,
not believed. There were welts on your back;
now they've gone.

You try to explain:

You had a belly once. You had a body.

This place stores you in the leg of a bird,

and not an invested one

but a chicken, pecking,

running lines in the ground.

Most of the time is gone.

You're a stream down which

a foundling comes.

You're a paramecium—

all the hints and holds of life

are here in you, but you

are just a little one.

You use yourself to laugh, clutch your chin

with one hand, rest the other on your knee.

You use yourself to say

no, I do not have scars—to clarify.

You use yourself like the chicken in the yard

uses itself to get by.

No one can say milk is bad.

Emerson, Gibran,
morals unsullied by religion.
Wholesome, white nectar that
reveals universal truth.

You've had sex: You're contaminated.

Milk can make you hygienic again if it's
inserted under the right conditions—
with threats, in a flowery and gaslit abyss.

When your parents visit, they gush.

> *Isn't it beautiful!*
> *Milk in the mountain, in the furniture, in the promenade!*
> *Milk in the fireplace, in the pond, in the wood!*

You open your mouth to explain—
the milk is a *burrito*, the milk is isolation,
sleep deprivation; the milk is *eyes down* while
a grown man or woman gets going, gets into
the spirit of the thing, slides their shoulders

squarely into the screaming, swearing, name-
calling, lying, manipulating, and shaming

—but your father puts his fingers to your lips.

> *Nothing you could possibly tell us*
> *could ever change our minds*
> *about any of this.*

The end of the family.
Even the wreckage is gone.

[new truth #3]

You will end your days comfortably,
with dachshunds at your feet, a fire
in the hearth, a lover at your side, and
six grateful children who earn good
money if (and only if) you describe
to your father in detail the time you
gave head to the Scottish boy while
he wore your grandfather's coat.
Leaving anything out will mean
you'll have to tell it to him again.

Listen.
I haven't hit you.
I've only demonstrated
the richness of your feeling
and the piracy inherent in your
unwillingness to
brave the feeling. I've only
pulled you up. I've only
sheltered you with a slap. I've
dipped into your orange blood
with my finger
and brought relief—I know
how to help. You listen to me—
your blood will redden,
and your face.
You'll get
better.

You run in place for hours
while he yells.

If you stop (or if you continue)
he'll make fun, pull out folktales
about your past, having read
(or having never read, as the
case may be) your *file*, that
anthology of things scavenged
from your room at home and
faxed to the institution.

                                                    [when they feed you the milk]

The man circles a field mouse
running under the gaze of her God.

                                                    [it may not

Everything you're doing is wrong

                                                    all go in]

—and now he says you're doing it right,
collapsed on the floor, vomit between the legs,
blood vessels breaking above the eyelids.

[the milk may make its way down]

He squats and shows you your bay,
filled with his ships. He has pieces
of advice which he'll cut off like fat
and throw to you now.

You'd better eat.

[the milk may run along the chin]

It's very early or very late.
A cassette plays the same song on repeat.

You each link your arms and legs.
Close the circle, says the woman.
Let no one in.

A fourteen-year-old boy stands
outside your teenage wall.
She circles him, a bird over bones,
and shouts commands—
he must *break in!*

But he's small for his age,
arms and wrists thin.
He tries to crawl, but you tighten.
He tries to climb, but you lean in
and close the top.
He flips upside down and hangs,
but cannot penetrate.

The woman scoffs.
Do you want to spend your whole life
on the outside, unloved and alone?

43

The blame is his that he can't break in,
though you are many and he is one.
He is hope
rent down the belly,
viscera drawn across
the 80s carpet.

His is vintage rage
burst from the barrel
then swallowed by sand
to absolutely no effect.

The tape stops. She speaks
one authoritative word
and breaks the human chain.
The lesson is clear:
the route to love is
through absolute power.

Now journal about this, she says.
Three pages, single spaced—
then you can lie on the floor
for half an hour.

You sit on the floor, writing on the seat of a chair.
They've told you to describe your *nightmare*.
Not a dream or a fear, but you at your worst.
Not a reasonable worst—not homeless, or dead.

    GO FARTHER
    DIG DEEPER
    BE HONEST
    DON'T SUGARCOAT IT
    I WANT TO KNOW

WHAT   ARE   YOU   CAPABLE   OF

The music concusses, the man screams—
you spin their wool—you can't not—
to find the worst imaginable thing—
only horror will pass muster,
gain you praise, make you safe—

so you write *I'd kill my children*

—and now begins the rest of your life
living with this.

You have a snake in your skin.

It pulls approval out
in the form of votes.
You're one of only three
to get enough.

You sit in the *lifeboat* and watch the rest.
They give you messages, then cry
as they drown in the brown rug.

You are stone.
You are before or after—
but hardly here.

You're behind the swell of the skin snake's
belly; she's pregnant with her kits,
glorying in this—
messiah complex,
survivor's guilt,
hematomas on the inner eye.

You're a garden rake turned golden comb.
All your endeavors must now succeed

—you *will* achieve. You cannot waste
the dead's faith.

Not a choice:

Three days in bandages and earplugs:
the Helen Keller. A girl unwraps him on stage.
All of you leer. It's not entertainment
(staff gave a disclaimer) but it is.
What will he be like when the veil lifts?
But he disappoints—he's stunned
by the lights, gives a monotonous
speech, leaves.

A week in a wheelchair. On the last night,
he stands up, speaks briefly, gets off the stage.
The best part of the show was beforehand
anyway, watching him struggle on a hillside
campus with no ramps.

A week of wearing a shirt with every name
hurled at him since childhood splashed in red
across his chest and arms and back. In the
dining room you've caught sight of him
by way of "FAILURE," "WORTHLESS,"

"FUCK-UP." He gives a speech, then strips,
throws the shirt into the fire. It's really
something else.

A mime in which he must play both his father and
his younger self. First he is the man, punching.
Then he is the child, falling, wailing. You had not
seen him cry before, but they've achieved it now,
fabulously, under stage lights. You all clap
as he collapses. The staff put their feet in the
stirrups; once broken, animals can be of use.

Not a choice—for girls:

Dress up as a two-year-old and sit on a blanket.

Hold stuffed animals and speak about innocence.

Dance attractively in a leotard.

Waltz in pyjamas alone and cry.

I told a kind woman who
worked in the kitchen
I'd write a song about her one day.

I haven't.
Her name was Janet.
She was older, had dyed red hair.
We washed dishes together.

She brought me some small relief
which I don't know how to sing.

Let this poem, then,
be hers,
dug into the earth
by its own weight.

[new truth #4]

Grass gives way with grace,
bending under weight—
but you don't bend. You break
under grown men's brutality,
grown women's scorn,
the commodification of love.

To be like grass, you must be rebuilt.
To be rebuilt, you must destroy yourself.

You sit in the grass by the pond.
Sunday afternoons used to be bad,
but now that you're older, guardrails
line the cliff—you have Sundays off,
can sit in the sun, do nothing.
(You're either in the theatre of hell,
or you do nothing, play card games,
watch cartoons on Saturday mornings,
movies on Sunday evenings.)

[we were children]

Screams drift from the buildings behind
and to your left—a relief, because
they aren't a threat.

At least, they probably aren't.

Your name *could* have come up
in one of those rooms
from a trench some child dug
for safety (you can't
and don't blame them).

It could be that even now, despite the calm
water and warm sun, your fate is being
planned; that soon you'll be drawn
into isolation and lists.
They may decide you've done
or been (or failed to do or be)
something. You will—perhaps
for months—be forced to guess
what it is. You'll confess, write
out your dirt, vomit out your filth,
beat it out of pillows. They can
and will withhold sleep, smiles,
laughter, eye contact, and all agency
from you. They can and will murder
your year. They can and will.

When you finally get out,
they'll make you vow never
to speak of what happened here.
By the time you realize
you should, they'll have been sued
out of existence, to rise again
elsewhere under inspiring names
evoking mountains, creeks,
the safety of a sunny Sunday
by a pond.

25 ways I'm dirty 25 ways I
lie every day 25 times I've
used others to get what I
wanted 25 ways I betrayed
my family 25 ways I
betrayed myself 10 ways I
chose my nightmare 10
ways I manipulate my
friends 25 times I turned
my back on love 10 ways I
am a faker 25 times I've
failed to give love to others
25 ways I plan to sabotage
this experience

In English Literature, you build
a model of Gilgamesh's boat
with popsicle sticks.

P.E. class is juggling—
that is, playing cards.

In History, each page of your notebook
has the same heading: today's date and

U.S. HISTORY

with nothing underneath,
and nothing on the next page
but another day's date and

U.S. HISTORY

—the man commands you to write it,
then rolls the A/V unit in.

Sometimes it's the beginning,

sometimes the end, but always

the same:

a war—a cliff scene—French colonists—Indians—string
symphonies—a war—a cliff scene—French colonists—Indians—
string symphonies—a war—a cliff scene—French colonists—
Indians—string symphonies—a war—a cliff scene—French
colonists—Indians—string symphonies—a war—a cliff scene—
French colonists—Indians—string symphonies—a war—a cliff
scene—French colonists—Indians—string symphonies—a war—a
cliff scene—French colonists—Indians—string symphonies

Although we'll lie you down

in a faux funeral

and make you write and read aloud

your obituary

and make you change your name

and blame you for your rape

and censor all your mail

and deny you medical care

and deny you sleep

and describe to you in detail

how we beat our kids

then make you tell us

57

how you were abused

and allow you one 15-minute phone call

every two weeks

and only with the people

who arranged all this—

though we will, in short,

do everything in our power

to help,

ultimately

we cannot do it for you:

You *must change your life.*

III.

TWENTY-THREE YEARS

I showed the Devil my scars

and at first he wasn't impressed

He said

show me your arms again

I released the hounds from my sleeves,

exposed the hills and water features

He said

I'll buy that

I told him he couldn't afford it

He said

I know the price:
you want peaceful sleep

and I'll give it to you—just

give me your arms

No, I said slowly

so he could understand

I don't want your sleep

I want

to have

what you want

and

never give it to you again

In the dream

you're at a mass suicide   you hold a serrated knife
over your head   your life depends on a really good
            excuse   they won't allow insubordination
    your friends are dragged away and shot   everyone
is getting killed by people who eat their kills   someone
            holds a shotgun to your head

                                    you prepare yourself
    you're in a kitchen slicing your arm like bread   a man
with a chainsaw   cuts pieces of his body off   they fall
    into a stream at his feet   he looks at you
                        you try to kill a man but he won't
die   a lion picks you all off one by one   you capture a
    tarantula and eat its head   a white car goes off a cliff
        the passengers laugh   then wail   you slit open
        the car's roof with a butter knife   vomit everywhere
                        their faces doll-like in death
    everyone you've ever known is dead   they're burying

themselves in a giant vault   throwing trash and pens

and apples at you from their mausoleum shelves

you watch a murder

filmed a hundred years ago   you could take it to the police

but it'd be pointless   no culprit left to punish

no friends left to weep

your seven-year-old self is imprisoned   she wants

to call the younger version of your mother   you follow

the wires along the wall   they've all been cut

you're a conscript

you don't know what you're fighting   what it looks like

or feels like   everyone is running   there's a flood

you're on a roof that's collapsing   you're on a phone

to your mother   *we're dying here*

she can't hear you over the water

she leads you

up a white staircase to a doctor

looks at you   on your knees   says

you're permanently dysfunctional

and leaves

You're stripped,
cleaned, and dried,
your excesses removed.
You're carried in pieces
into an office to be registered.
You wait in an alcove
to be secured. You're gross,
not allowed to floss.
You're told you must stay
for two, four, or all foreseeable
years. You've been bad,
though it's vague. You're to be
punished, and it's proof
of your failure that you
don't know what for.

But this is all—you explain—
a mistake,
a misunderstanding
between adults.

But it is not.
You are stored away and locked.

You gum the doctor's coattail
and kiss and scream
as he explains:

> *You don't know what you need.*
> *You never did.*

A mere hair, he plucks you.
Then you're shelved.

You fall, go on
all fours
from hall to hall,
belly up when
you find a nurse.

She assures you
those sensible herds
trampled you because
you lay in the path of
progress:

> *The doctor is quite right—*
> *you must quit your life.*

She leaves you at the altar,
her white dress and all hope
receding, heedless of your
many deaths.

You've been here decades.
You're nearly done. But
the man won't let you sleep,
and you lose control—you rage—

—then take it back, become logic's gem, reason's bride,
but it's too late. Emotion
has been shown. You have a will
of your own; you must be
tamped down, redone;
the first time
didn't take.

He turns and smiles,
begins to speak.
In his open mouth,

      tongue
      teeth
      uvula

hell—

[new truth #5]

This is clear:

When the sentence the term the life is over,
the many dead—

hanged, crashed, shot, diagnosed, undiagnosed, overdosed

—don't have to go home,
but they can't stay here.

In the dream,
you're leaving.
You sit with the man
in a final meeting.

Your plan:
When you get off his land,
you will spit.

You'll aim for his feet.

(But you could *never*—you'll make sure it hits the ground instead.)

You wake before
you can dare.

You
cannot
show
                         (cannot dare to show)

anything
but gratitude,
milk running down your chin.

Silly little girl
doesn't realise her world is
being bombed refuses to accept
she is about to die as she
breathes in all the little ashes
chokes but silly little girl
stomps her foot and ignores the
cries around her, hands grabbing
her ankles everyone is sinking
but silly little girl won't go
down won't go down she won't
go down denies the dark green
clouds as the air is replaced
with nothing just closes her
eyes if I can't see them
they can't see me if I can't
see them they can't see me
if I can't see them they can't
see me and she believes it
all silly little girl she
really believes it all refuses
to accept she is about to die
and the silly little girl is the
last one to go down

Written by the author in 1997, age 16, at Rocky Mountain
Academy – CEDU Family of Services, Bonners Ferry, ID.

Further Resources

Journalist and author Maia Szalavitz describes the lucrative and abusive "troubled teen" industry in great detail in her 2006 book, *Help at Any Cost: How the Troubled Teen Industry Cons Parents and Hurts Kids* (Riverhead Books).

Breaking Code Silence is a survivor-run nonprofit organization aimed at tackling the "Troubled Teen Industry." Through advocacy, awareness, research, and legislation, Breaking Code Silence is building a network of survivor resources and funds to begin taking on these facilities and those at the helm of the abuse.
www.breakingcodesilence.org

Acknowledgments

"new truth #1" was published as "Because God loves the wasp" in *Cold Lake Anthology: 2018 Writing from the Burlington Writers Workshop*, 2018.

"The English boy dwells in," "Listen," and "How it feels is a series of questions" were published in *Feminist Studies*, Vol. 45, No. 1, May 2019.

About the Press

Unsolicited Press was founded in 2012 and is based in Portland, Oregon. The small press publishes fiction, poetry, and creative nonfiction written by award-winning and emerging authors. Some of its authors include Jackson Bliss, Brook Bhagat, Mick Bennett, Margaret DeRitter, John W. Bateman, Anne Leigh Parrish, Adrian Ernesto Cepeda, and Raki Kopernik.

Learn more at www.unsolicitedpress.com

Follow us on instagram and twitter: @unsolicitedp